~~The~~ my MÜTTER MUSEUM

Welcome! Come on in!

A J's Junior Guide's Tour of the Coolest Me... Coolest Me...

Written by Anna Dhody   Illustrated by Ted E... ...era

Schiffer**Kids**

4880 Lower Valley Road, Atglen, PA 19310

Other Schiffer Books on Related Subjects:
Sticks 'n' Stones 'n' Dinosaur Bones: Being a Whimsical Take on a (pre)Historical Event, by Ted Enik and G. F. Newland, ISBN 978-0-7643-5394-9
The Bathysphere Boys: The Depth-Defying Diving of Messrs. Beebe and Barton, by Ted Enik and G. F. Newland, ISBN 978-0-7643-5793-0

Cover design by Brenda McCallum
Type set in Athelas/Pulpo/Garfield Antique

ISBN: 978-0-7643-5988-0
Printed in China

Co-published by Pixel Mouse House & Schiffer Publishing, Ltd.
4880 Lower Valley Road
Atglen, PA 19310
Phone: (610) 593-1777; Fax: (610) 593-2002
E-mail: Info@schifferbooks.com
Web: www.schifferbooks.com

For our complete selection of fine books on this and related subjects, please visit our website at www.schifferbooks.com. You may also write for a free catalog.

Schiffer Publishing's titles are available at special discounts for bulk purchases for sales promotions or premiums. Special editions, including personalized covers, corporate imprints, and excerpts, can be created in large quantities for special needs. For more information, contact the publisher.

We are always looking for people to write books on new and related subjects. If you have an idea for a book, please contact us at proposals@schifferbooks.com.

Letter from the Curator

Many years ago, a young girl walked slowly into the Mütter Museum. She gripped her mother's hand tightly, looking nervous, scared, and maybe a bit excited. She kept her eyes on the dark-red carpet, until her mother squeezed her hand. Slowly the young girl looked up, her eyes got wide, her skin went pale; then she turned and dragged her mother out of the museum.

My mom and I watched them hurry past, shrugged to each other, and went back to reading about human horns. The point I'm trying to make is that the Mütter Museum isn't for everybody. And that's okay.

Hopefully, you are reading this book because you are interested in science, medicine, and the human body in general. I'm often asked if we have age restrictions at the Mütter. No, we don't; in fact, I've had a seven-year-old ask me some amazing questions, and seen adults run out in a panic. It isn't about the age of your body, but the level of interest in your mind.

Generally, I've found that the best time to visit the museum is when you start learning about the different parts and systems of the human body. It's then that the collection takes on new meaning, and you can really begin to understand how far medicine has advanced over the past 150 years.

I've included a section in the back of the book with more information on each specimen or object we visit. The Mütter Museum's collection is made up of more than 25,000 different skeletons, wet specimens, wax models, instruments, and so on. Each is unique, but all serve the same purpose: education. That has been our mission since the museum opened in 1863. And while this book has a whimsical feel, we take care to always remember, honor, and respect the people whose bodies we care for. To me, they are more than specimens; they are family.

I hope you enjoy reading this book as much as I've enjoyed writing it for you.

Your friend and curator,

Anna Dhody

Hi! WELCOME TO THE MÜTTER MUSEUM

FOLLOW ME!

Birthplace of American Medicine

I'm A.J., a junior guide here–actually, I'm the most junior junior guide!

C'mon, let me show you around and tell you about some of my favorite things. Cool.

Did you know the Mütter Museum is part of a much larger medical society: the College of Physicians of Philadelphia? No, not that kind of college. It doesn't give out medical degrees or anything. It's more like a group of doctors got together a really, really long time ago— way back in 1787—to form a special society all about promoting health.

So, why is it called the Mütter Museum? Not "mutter," like when you mumble under your breath. Look over here at the sign. See the "u" in 'Mütter?' It's got these two little dots over it. That's called an umlaut; it changes the way you pronounce the "u" from an "uh" sound to an "oo." Rhyme our name with scooter and you'll be fine!

And I have no idea why the word "umlaut" doesn't have an umlaut in it . . . but we really should get going.

Okay, now that we know how to pronounce his name, we can stop and say hi to Dr. Thomas Dent Mütter.

After all, he's why it's called the Mütter Museum! In 1859, Dr. Mütter donated his entire collection of teaching stuff to the college, along with a bunch of money to create a museum. And lots of his original specimens are still here on display more than 150 years later!

But for now, let's start with the first person you see when you enter the museum. Preee-senting, the one and only Soap Lady!

No, she's not actually made of soap. Then why do we call her that? Hang on, I'll get to it. Here she is. Now, lot's of people think she's a mummy. But she's not technically "mummified," she's "soponified."

That means, after she died her body went through some chemical changes that morphed all her fat into something called adipocere. Since this adipocere is waxy, fatty, soapy-like stuff, we just call her the Soap Lady.

While she is not an original part of Mütter's donation, the Soap Lady has been with us since 1874.

And against the wall there is the Hyrtl Skull Collection . . .

... 139 skulls from the collection of Dr. Joseph Hyrtl. He put it together more than 150 years ago to convince other doctors and scientists that you couldn't judge how smart a person was or if they were good or bad just by checking out the shape and size of their skull.

Back then, doctors were really doing this. It was called phrenology, and Dr. Hyrtl thought it didn't make sense. So he collected all these skulls and facts about where they came from to prove that phrenology was wrong.

Next up? A French woman who, um, knew how to make a point. Follow me.

Say "Hello-Bonjour (Bone-joor!)" to Madame Dimanche, or the Widow Sunday.

Now, this is a wax model, but the madame was real, and she lived in Paris in the 1800s. And that horn actually grew out of her head. Except for one thing . . . it's not a horn! It's called a cornu cutaneum, and it's just a part of her skin that grew out of control.

Let's go downstairs; there's a bunch more to see!

This is the Mütter's American Giant. He's 7 feet, 6 inches tall and the second-tallest skeleton on display in the entire world. The tallest is only one measly inch taller. I happen to know that our curator—she's in charge of the museum's objects here—is a little bit cranky about this fact.

Here, look at his spine. See how crooked? He had scoliosis, kyphosis, and lordosis! These are all types of curvatures of the spine that can shrink a person. Our curator says, with all that twistiness, his articulation (ar-tic-u-lay-shun: the way he was put back together) may be off, and he could have stood over 7 feet, 7 inches tall.

But there's no way to prove it. The good news is, his femurs are the longest in the world! P.S.: your femurs are your thigh bones.

Now, right next to the Giant is Mary Ashberry, and she had a condition known as dwarfism.

There are more than 200 different types of dwarfism, and Mary definitely had the most common; achondroplasia.
It's a genetic condition that occurs in about 1 out of 40,000 children
and causes about 70 percent of all the known cases of dwarfism.

C'mon, let's say hi to Harry.

This is Harry Eastlack. He's the only fully articulated skeleton on display in North America with fibrodysplasia ossificans progressiva, or FOP. This is a really, really rare disease. There are only about 900 diagnosed cases in the entire world. FOP is another genetic condition, which means one you're born with. It causes bone to grow in places it's not supposed to.

Where? Well, take a good look at Harry. What do you see? Do his bones look normal to you?

Right! All that extra bone! Now look again, and tell me what you don't see! I'll give you a hint; look back at the Mütter American Giant.

You see all the metal screws and wire and stuff used to keep him in one piece? Now look at Harry . . . Right! Hardly any hardware at all. Why? Because his skeleton completely fused together before he died. There's currently no cure for FOP, but scientists are close to a treatment, and hopefully it'll come out soon.

So far, we've been looking mostly at "weird illnesses" and "because-of-your-genes" conditions—things that happen to your body, and things you're born with. But what about things you do to yourself?

Another one of Dr. Mütter's original specimens is this skeleton here. Look closely at her. You notice anything unusual? We put this normal-looking skeleton in the same case so you can compare. So, what's going on?

Yes! Her rib cage is messed up. Look how squished it is. But, guess what? This isn't caused by any disease or genetic condition. This happened because of clothes! Many years ago, some women wore a kind of underwear called a corset. It gave them back support, and if you laced it up tight it would make your waist tiny. But it also caused problems like . . . Well, tummy trouble. Yeah, farting.

We should keep moving along . . . so much to see, so little time! Do you want to meet Chang and Eng? Follow me.

Well okay, this isn't really them. It's just a cast of . . . Chang and Eng Bunker! You ever heard of "Siamese twins"? We don't say that anymore; we use the term "conjoined twins" when two kids are born attached to each other. That's them, right down there.

Chang and Eng were born in Siam (now Thailand) in 1811 and are one of the most famous pairs of conjoined twins in all of history. They performed in circuses and sideshows and eventually had their own traveling company. They toured all over the world . . .

. . . but eventually settled in North Carolina, married two sisters, and together had twenty-one children! Chang and Eng lived to be sixty-two years old. After they died, the doctors examined their bodies and discovered that the twins were connected by the liver—wow!

Did you know the liver is part of the digestive system? And, speaking of digesting, would you like to see the world's largest colon? Yeah, right. I thought so. C'mon, it's this way.

Behold! Congenital aganglionic megacolon caused by Hirschsprung's disease! But we just call it megacolon.

The "mega" part is obvious; it's 8 feet, 4 inches long, and more than a foot and a half wide! The normal grownup's colon, the large intestine, is only about 5 feet long. Hirschsprung's disease causes constant constipation, because parts of the colon shut down and it can't get rid of the waste. This guy lived to be twenty-nine, and when he died they took out 40 pounds of poo.

Hey! Come back! It's only stuffed with straw.

Okay, okay, sorry. Let's take a break and see something nonbiological. You know, nothing human, but still cool.

Open these drawers. Go on, open them. This is the Chevalier Jackson Collection— more than 2,000 objects that got stuck in people's throats. Hey, I said they weren't human. I didn't say they weren't disturbing!

But listen, Dr. Jackson was a really interesting guy. He personally removed every single one of these things, then wrote down everything about each operation. Then he organized that info into categories, see? Toys, Jewelry, Food, Hardware, and Pins. Tons of pins.

He even invented special tools to remove stuff from people's throats without surgery!

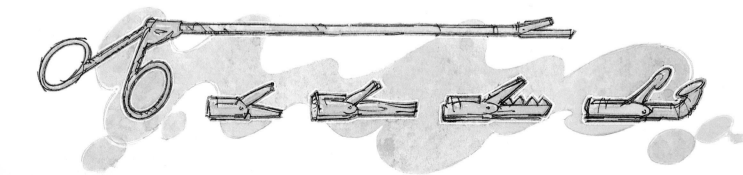

Wow, that was fast! Nearly closing time. We're almost at the end of our tour.

But there's still one super-famous, important person you really have to meet. Well, one important part of him, anyway. Follow me!

You wanna see Albert Einstein's brain? Here it is. Right here! Um . . . not all of it, just some. Those slides are thin sections of Einstein's actual brain.

We have forty-six of them, made just after Einstein died in 1955. Why? Well, people think Einstein was one of the greatest minds of all time . . .

. . . and they wanted to study his brain to see if anything was special or different in there that made him so smart.

So far, nothing. But people are still looking—and arguing about it.

Okay. Now I really gotta say goodbye. But I hope you had a great tour, and when you come back again I'll show you even more of my favorites! There's always something new to learn and get excited about here. See you!

Oops! Here comes my mom. I should have told you she's the curator here. She gave me a job to do and I forgot.

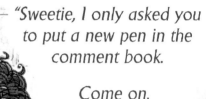

"Sweetie, I only asked you to put a new pen in the comment book.

Come on, let's go do it together."

"A.J., the guard says you gave another tour."

"But they were about my age, Mama, and we had a great time. At least I think so. Nobody fainted . . . this visit."

"I'm so proud of you. But you know something? You aren't just my littlest guide anymore."

"I'm not?! Why?"

"'Cause I think you're the museum's BEST guide!"

Philadelphia / The College of Physicians of Philadelphia

The city of Philadelphia is called the Birthplace of American Medicine™ because it established the first hospital and first medical school in the country. Even today, one out of every six medical students in the United States comes through Philadelphia at some point during their training. That's a lot of doctors! The College of Physicians of Philadelphia is one of the oldest medical professional societies in America! And it is still very active in its mission, which is:
advancing the cause of health while upholding the ideals and heritage of medicine.

The Soap Lady

The Soap Lady has an interesting story. When she first came to us in 1874, we thought her name was Mrs. Ellenbogen, that she died during a yellow fever epidemic in Philadelphia in 1792, and that she was the grandmother of one of our fellows, Dr. Joseph Leidy (fellows are members of the college). We thought this because he said she was. However, in the 1940s the curator at the time, Dr. McFarland, wanted to find proof of Leidy's claim. He looked at death records, church logs, and all sorts of documents and found out that (a) there was no yellow fever epidemic in 1792 (in 1793, yes), and (b) there was nobody named Ellenbogen living in Philadelphia then! Also, in 1986 we x-rayed her body and found straight pins (probably used to pin a burial shroud around her) that were not manufactured until the 1830s! So Dr. Leidy was lying; she wasn't his grandmother after all. But then who was the Soap Lady? We're still trying to figure that out, using 21st-century science and

The Hyrtl Skulls

If you look closely at each skull, you can see where Dr. Hyrtl wrote down information about the person it belonged to. Now look closer . . . see how unique they are? Your skull is part of what makes up your face, and your face is special, right? Well, so are these skulls; each one is different from the rest. Dr. Hyrtl was very passionate, and his opinions were not popular at the time. He argued that with so much difference between individuals, how could a person be judged based on their ancestry? Eventually, Hyrtl was forced to retire from the University of Vienna and sell off much of his prized collections. The Mütter purchased the Hyrtl skulls in 1874. Today, they've all been CT scanned, and scientists from around the world, and in many different fields, have studied this valuable research collection.

alicia
van Antoniewicz, age 26

1006.139

Island of Lissa, Dalmatia
Orazio Trani, age 39
Idiot

Frontal grooves.

1006..133

Girolamo Zini, age 20
Rope-walker. Died of atlanto-axial
dislocation (broken neck).

Istria, Trieste (Italy)

1006.120

Joseph Donat, age 30
Brewer. Died of edema of the lungs.
Mental tubercles and chin shape.

Pinzgau, Austria

Madame Dimanche

A cornu cutaneum is made up of the same kind of material as your hair and nails. It took more than nine years for her horn to grow to this size, and eventually doctors convinced Madame Dimanche to have it removed. People can still get these cornu cutaneums today. It is linked to sun exposure, so put on that sunscreen!

The Mütter American Giant

Basically, there are two ways you can be tall. You can be genetically tall: if your parents and grandparents are tall, chances are you're going to be tall. But you can also be pathologically tall. That means, something weird happens in your body that forces it to become super tall—like what happened to the Mütter American Giant. He has something called pituitary gigantism. This condition is caused by the overproduction of growth hormones in childhood. With pituitary gigantism, you keep growing and growing until your body can't take it anymore. By looking at his skeleton, we can tell that he was in his early twenties when he died. And while this is something we can treat today, there was nothing that could help him in the 1800s.

Mary Ashberry

Technically, Mary's dwarfism isn't what killed her. We know that Mary died trying to give birth. In 1856 having a baby could be dangerous for any woman, but it was especially so for someone with dwarfism. Mary's birth canal was too small, and sadly, her baby got stuck and died. So a cesarean section—where an incision is made in the abdomen and uterus—was performed. It's a fairly common procedure today, but imagine having one done without anesthesia! And doctors didn't know what caused infection at that time, so it's likely they didn't wash their hands or instruments, which is probably why Mary died of an infection a few days later (in 1856). The good news is, thanks to medical advancements, women with dwarfism can now deliver children safely.

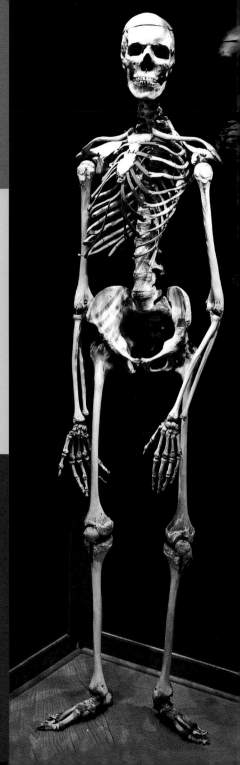

Harry Eastlack

With FOP (fibrodysplasia ossificans progressiva), not only does extra bone grow all over the skeleton, it grows in and around the joints too, fusing them together. This is a very painful disease that gradually freezes a person in place. There is no cure or even an approved treatment. But there's some good news; scientists are conducting promising drug trials.

The Corset Skeleton

In the mid-1800s, some women wore tight-laced corsets all the time, even to sleep! A tiny waist was considered highly attractive in those days, so many women, mainly in the United States and Europe, did this. But it came at a cost. When the rib cage is compressed, the internal organs are affected. You can't take a deep breath—in fact, sometimes the lower lungs can't work properly at all. And it's hard to eat with a tight corset squishing the intestines down and causing digestive problems. It was later discovered that wearing tight corsets can actually alter the shape of skeletons! This skeleton was part of Dr. Mütter's original donation. We recently found out that this skeleton's ribs may not actually have been deformed by a corset! Some scholars believe that the skeleton's shape is more consistent with corset styles from the 1890s, long after Dr. Mütter died. So something else may have caused the ribs to look like this. But what? We don't know yet, but we will continue to look into this.

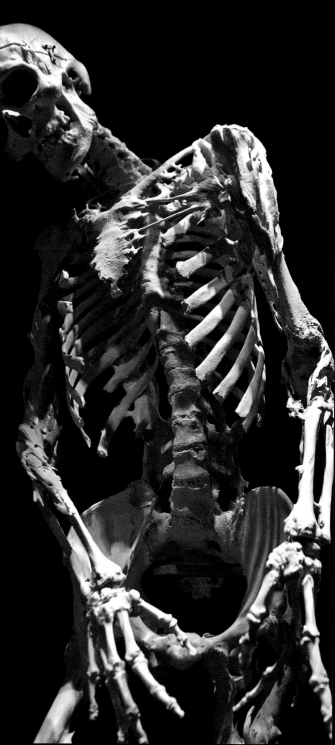

Chang and Eng

Chang and Eng really wanted to be separated, but they knew it was a very risky operation—especially in the 1800s! Just before they got married, the twins decided to go ahead with the surgery, but their wives-to-be convinced them it was far too dangerous. After the brothers died in 1874, doctors examined their bodies and found that they had attached livers. This meant that they probably would have died if they attempted the separation surgery. If Chang and Eng lived today, odds are they could be separated successfully.

The Megacolon

Congenital aganglionic megacolon (Hirschsprung's disease) is a congenital condition; you are born with it. The nerves that are supposed to form around your colon fail to develop, and this causes . . . well, a traffic jam. Waste material can't move properly through the large intestines, and it gets backed up and chronic constipation ensues. The owner of this colon—we know him as J.W.— lived to be twenty-nine years old but started having constipation at eighteen months of age. Over the years, his belly expanded and his organs moved to make room for his enlarged intestines. Toward the end of his life, he moved his bowels only about once a month! Today we can treat Hirschsprung's disease with surgery. Many people with the condition now live long and healthy lives.

Albert Einstein

Most researchers agree that even though Einstein was seventy-six when he died, his brain looks like a young man's. Why is that? We don't know. There's only so much you can learn about the brain by looking at it. We do know that Einstein's brain lacked significant lipofuscin (a fatty brownish substance that forms in the brain as we age), but we don't know if that was relevant to his intelligence. There are at least four other boxes of Einstein brain slides out there, but as of now, the Mütter Museum is the only place where the public can see an actual piece of Einstein's brain on permanent display.

Dr. Chevalier Jackson

We have drawers and drawers of safety pins. Except Dr. Jackson referred to them as danger pins! He was known as the Father of Endoscopy. That's a nonsurgical way of looking into your body and performing various procedures—like removing these objects. Before Dr. Jackson developed his instruments and techniques, patients often had to have major surgery. Those operations could take hours, but Jackson could often remove an object in minutes. We know this because he timed every procedure!

Souvenir
of Clinical
Congress
(Southwest)
Kansas City

Chevalier Jackson

Carol Orzel

On February 28, 2019, Harry got a roommate. Her name was Carol Orzel, and like Harry, she had FOP. Carol saw Harry's skeleton at an FOP conference in 1995, and from that moment on, she knew that when her time came, she too, wanted to be on display at the Mütter Museum. In life, Carol was a passionate advocate for FOP research. She never hesitated to educate people about FOP. When Carol saw Harry's skeleton, she realized that she also had the ability to continue educating people in death. Carol passed away on February 26, 2018, at the age of fifty-eight. With the help of her physician, Frederick Kaplan, her care facility, the Inglis House, and many other amazing people who rallied to honor Carol, we were able to fulfill her final wish. Carol did have one requirement for donation; she said we had to also accept her jewelry collection, so that her bling could be displayed with her. We were happy to do so.

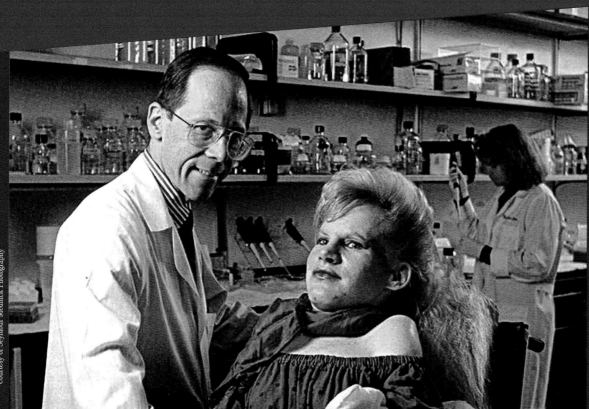

Acknowledgments

The author wishes to thank her mother for bringing her to the Mütter Museum when she was far too young, and for never, ever, telling her to act normal. She also wishes to thank all of her amazing colleagues at the College of Physicians of Philadelphia for their time and patience. This book would not be possible without the love, support, and childcare of her friends and family; she owes them big time. And finally, to the thousands of children who come to the museum every year: you are the scientists, physicians, innovators, and dreamers of the future. The world is yours, sorry about that.

To my beloved A.J.s.
The one I married.
The one I birthed.
And all the "A.J.s" who see themselves
in this book.
A.D.

To my one-of-a-kindred, extended family of "Morbids."
Without the lucky all of that, I'd likely not be part of this.
T.E.

To my wife and children, who quietly cheer me on every day.
R.A.H.

Thomas Dent Mütter (1811–1859)

Professor of Surgery

IN THE JEFFERSON MEDICAL COLLEGE OF PHILADELPHIA